# The Perfect Potato Salad Cookbook

© Copyright 2023. Laura Sommers.
All rights reserved.
No part of this book may be reproduced in any form or by any electronic or mechanical means without written permission of the author. All text, illustrations and design are the exclusive property of
Laura Sommers

| | |
|---|---|
| Introduction | 1 |
| How To Boil Potatoes | 2 |
| How To Bake Potatoes | 3 |
| How To Grill Potatoes | 4 |
| Classic Potato Salad | 5 |
| Classic Red Potato Salad | 6 |
| German Potato Salad | 7 |
| Homestyle Potato Salad | 8 |
| Sweet Potato Salad | 9 |
| Loaded Baked Potato Salad | 10 |
| Waldorf Potato Salad | 11 |
| Egg Pickle Potato Salad | 12 |
| Sweet Relish Potato Salad | 13 |
| Crab Boil Potato Salad | 14 |
| Lobster Potato Salad | 15 |
| Curry Potato Salad | 16 |
| Ranch Potato Salad | 17 |
| Bacon Ranch Potato Salad | 18 |
| Chipotle Ranch Potato Salad | 19 |
| Garden Potato Salad | 20 |
| Ham and Cheese Potato Salad | 21 |
| Green Goddess Potato Salad | 22 |
| Avocado Shrimp Potato Salad | 23 |

| | |
|---|---|
| Coleslaw Potato Salad | 24 |
| Dill Potato Salad | 25 |
| Beet Dill Potato Salad | 26 |
| Nordic Potato Salad | 27 |
| Dutch Potato Salad | 28 |
| Peruvian Potato Salad | 29 |
| Chicken Potato Salad | 30 |
| Herb Vinegar Potato Salad | 31 |
| Tomato Potato Salad | 32 |
| French Potato Salad | 33 |
| Niçoise Potato Salad | 34 |
| Provençal Potato Salad | 35 |
| Pesto Pea Potato Salad | 36 |
| Patriotic Potato Salad | 37 |
| Pico de Gallo Potato Salad | 38 |
| Salsa Verde Potato Salad | 39 |
| Sichuan Potato Salad | 40 |
| Carrot Sesame Potato Salad | 41 |
| Salt Cod Potato Salad | 42 |
| Thai Potato Salad | 43 |
| Indian Potato Salad | 44 |
| Greek Potato Salad | 45 |
| Caviar Potato Salad | 46 |
| Amish Potato Salad | 47 |

Honey Mustard Potato Salad ................................................... 48

Classic American Style Potato Salad ...................... 49

Garden Potato Salad .............................................................. 50

Veggie Potato Salad ............................................................... 51

Blue Cheese and Bacon Potato Salad ............................. 52

Dill Potato Salad ....................................................................... 53

Italian Potato Salad ................................................................ 54

Roasted New Potato Salad .................................................. 55

Herbed Potato Salad .............................................................. 56

Lemon Potato Salad ............................................................... 57

Spanish Potato Salad ............................................................. 58

Ranch Potato Salad ................................................................ 59

Red Potato Salad ..................................................................... 60

Oktoberfest Potato Salad ..................................................... 61

Canadian Potato Salad .......................................................... 63

Caribbean Potato Salad ........................................................ 65

Buttermilk No Mayonnaise Potato Salad ....................... 66

Red No Mayo Potato Salad .................................................. 67

Southern Dill Potato Salad .................................................. 68

Curried Potato Salad .............................................................. 69

Maryland Potato Salad .......................................................... 71

Carolina Potato Salad ............................................................ 72

Bacon and Chipotle Potato Salad ..................................... 73

Bayou Potato Salad ................................................................ 74

**Bacon Sriracha Potato Salad** ............................................... 75
**Buffalo Potato Salad** .......................................................... 76
**About the Author** ............................................................... 77
**Other Books by Laura Sommers** ........................................ 78

# Introduction

Potato salad is a classic dish that has been enjoyed for generations. Whether it's at a family barbecue, a potluck, or just as a side dish for dinner, potato salad always adds a touch of comfort and nostalgia to any meal. With so many variations and regional specialties, potato salad is a dish that can be made to suit any taste preference. Some like it creamy and tangy, while others prefer it with a more classic, mustard-based dressing. Some like it warm, and others prefer it cold. No matter how you like your potato salad, there is something for everyone.

In this cookbook, we have compiled a collection of the best potato salad recipes from around the world. From the classic American-style potato salad to the creamy and rich German potato salad, we have recipes for every palate. We have also included some unique and unexpected twists on the classic dish, like a sweet potato and apple salad or a roasted garlic and herb potato salad. Whether you're looking for a side dish for your next barbecue or just something to enjoy for a weeknight dinner, we hope that this cookbook will inspire you to try something new and delicious. So grab a fork, dig in, and enjoy!

# How To Boil Potatoes

1. Fill a pot with enough water to just cover the potatoes.
2. Turn the burner on high and bring water to boiling.
3. Reduce heat to medium low or low.
4. Cover the pan with a lid.
5. Cook the potatoes in gently boiling water until tender, about 15 minutes for cubed potatoes and new potatoes and 20 to 25 minutes for quartered potatoes.
6. It is easier to peel the potatoes after they are cooked, but they will cook faster if you peel them before hand.

# How To Bake Potatoes

## Ingredients:

4 medium-sized russet potatoes
1 tbsp. olive oil
Salt and pepper, to taste

## Directions:

1. Preheat your oven to 400 degrees F (205°C).
2. Scrub the potatoes thoroughly to remove any dirt or debris, then pat them dry with a clean towel.
3. Using a fork, prick each potato several times all over. This will allow steam to escape as the potatoes bake, preventing them from bursting open in the oven.
4. Rub each potato with olive oil, making sure to coat them evenly.
5. Sprinkle with salt and pepper to taste.
6. Place the potatoes on a baking sheet or in a baking dish.
7. Bake the potatoes for 45-60 minutes, or until they are tender when pierced with a fork.
8. The baking time will depend on the size of your potatoes, so it's a good idea to check them periodically starting around the 45-minute mark.
9. Remove the potatoes from the oven and allow them to cool for a few minutes before serving.

# How To Grill Potatoes

1. Preheat your grill to medium-high heat.
2. Slice the potatoes into 1/4 inch rounds or wedges.
3. Toss the potato slices with olive oil, salt, pepper, and any other desired seasonings.
4. Arrange the potato slices in a single layer on a grill basket or directly on the grill grates.
5. Grill the potatoes for about 5-7 minutes on each side, or until they are tender and lightly charred.
6. Remove the potatoes from the grill and serve hot.

Note: Cooking time may vary depending on the thickness of the potato slices and the heat of the grill. Be sure to keep an eye on them while they're cooking to prevent burning.

# Classic Potato Salad

## Ingredients:

2 pounds russet potatoes
2 tbsps. cider vinegar
1/2 tsp. salt, or to taste
2 cups mayonnaise
2 scallions, diced
1 celery stalk, diced
1 tbsp. Dijon mustard
1 tbsp. vinegar
1 tsp. sugar

## Directions:

1. Boil, peel and cube the potatoes.
2. Toss with vinegar and salt.
3. Whisk together mayonnaise, scallions, celery, mustard, vinegar and sugar.
4. Salt to taste.
5. Pour over the potatoes.
6. Gently stir to combine.
7. Chill if desired.
8. Serve and enjoy!

# Classic Red Potato Salad

## Ingredients:

2 pounds red potatoes
2 tbsps. cider vinegar
1/2 tsp. salt, or to taste
2 cups mayonnaise
2 scallions, diced
1 celery stalk, diced
1 tbsp. Dijon mustard
1 tbsp. vinegar
1 tsp. sugar

## Directions:

1. Boil, peel and cube the potatoes.
2. Toss with vinegar and salt.
3. Whisk together mayonnaise, scallions, celery, mustard, vinegar and sugar.
4. Salt to taste.
5. Pour over the potatoes.
6. Gently stir to combine.
7. Chill if desired.
8. Serve and enjoy!

# German Potato Salad

## Ingredients:

4 pounds potatoes, peeled and sliced thin
8 slices bacon
1/4 cup vegetable oil
1/2 cup finely chopped onion
1/2 cup white vinegar
1/4 cup water
1/3 cup sugar
1 tsp. salt
3 tbsp. finely chopped fresh parsley

## Directions:

1. In a large pot of boiling water, cook potatoes 10 to 15 minutes, or until fork-tender.
2. Drain.
3. Place in a large bowl, and set aside.
4. In a large skillet over medium heat, cook bacon until browned and crisp.
5. Drain on paper towels.
6. Crumble, and set aside.
7. Add oil and onion to bacon grease and cook 4 to 5 minutes, or until onion is soft.
8. Stir in vinegar, water, sugar and salt.
9. Bring to a boil.
10. Gently stir in potatoes and parsley.
11. Add half of bacon to potato mixture and heat until warmed through, stirring occasionally.
12. Remove to a serving dish, sprinkle remaining bacon over top.
13. Serve and enjoy!

# Homestyle Potato Salad

## Ingredients:

4 lbs. white or red potatoes
10 hard-cooked eggs, peeled and chopped
1/2 green or red bell pepper, diced
3 stalks celery, chopped
1 cup reduced-fat sour cream
1 cup light mayonnaise
1 tbsp. white vinegar
2 tbsps. nonfat milk
1 tbsp. sugar
1 tsp. salt
1/2 tsp. black pepper

## Directions:

1. Place potatoes in a large soup pot.
2. Cover with water, and bring to a boil over high heat.
3. Cook 25 to 30 minutes, or until fork-tender.
4. Drain and cool slightly.
5. Cut potatoes into chunks and place in a large bowl.
6. Add egg, bell pepper, and celery; set aside.
7. In a medium bowl, combine the remaining ingredients.
8. Mix well.
9. Pour sour cream mixture over potatoes and mix until thoroughly combined.
10. Chill 2 to 3 hours before serving.
11. Serve and enjoy!

# Sweet Potato Salad

## Ingredients:

5 sweet potatoes, peeled and cut into 1-inch chunks
1 cup mayonnaise
1/4 cup honey
1 tbsp. yellow mustard
1/2 cup raisins
1/2 cup chopped walnuts
1/4 tsp. salt

## Directions:

1. Place potatoes in a large saucepan and add just enough water to cover.
2. Bring to a boil over high heat and let boil 12 to 15 minutes, or until fork-tender then drain.
3. In a large bowl, combine remaining ingredients.
4. Mix well.
5. Add sweet potatoes and mix until well coated.
6. Cover and chill for at least 2 hours before serving.
7. Serve and enjoy!

# Loaded Baked Potato Salad

## Ingredients:

3 pounds small red potatoes
1 tbsp. olive oil
Kosher salt and freshly ground black pepper
1/2 pound bacon, diced
1 cup mayonnaise
1/2 cup sour cream
1/4 cup chopped fresh chives
1/4 cup chopped fresh parsley
1 tbsp. apple cider vinegar
1 tbsp. Dijon mustard
2 cups shredded cheddar cheese

## Directions:

1. Preheat the oven to 400 degrees F.
2. Cut the potatoes into 1-inch pieces and toss with the olive oil, 1 tsp. salt and a few grinds of black pepper on a baking sheet.
3. Roast until tender, about 30 minutes.
4. Meanwhile, cook the bacon in a large skillet over medium heat until crispy.
5. Remove with a slotted spoon to a paper towel-lined plate.
6. In a large bowl, whisk together the mayonnaise, sour cream, chives, parsley, vinegar, mustard, 1 tsp. salt and a few grinds of black pepper.
7. Add the potatoes, bacon and cheese to the bowl and toss to combine.
8. Serve warm or at room temperature.

# Waldorf Potato Salad

## Ingredients:

2 pounds russet potatoes
2 tbsps. cider vinegar
1/2 tsp. salt, or to taste
2 cups mayonnaise
2 scallions, diced
2 celery stalks, diced
1 tbsp. vinegar
1 tsp. sugar
1 chopped apple
1/2 cup chopped walnuts

## Directions:

1. Boil, peel and cube the potatoes.
2. Toss with apples, walnuts, vinegar and salt.
3. Whisk together mayonnaise, scallions, celery, vinegar and sugar.
4. Salt to taste.
5. Pour over the potatoes.
6. Gently stir to combine.
7. Chill if desired.
8. Serve and enjoy!

# Egg Pickle Potato Salad

## Ingredients:

2 pounds russet potatoes
2 tbsps. cider vinegar
1/2 tsp. salt, or to taste
2 cups mayonnaise
2 scallions, diced
1 celery stalk, diced
1 tbsp. Dijon mustard
1 tbsp. pickle juice
1 tsp. sugar
3 hard boiled eggs, chopped
1/2 cup bell pepper, chopped
1/4 cup pickle, diced

## Directions:

1. Boil, peel and cube the potatoes.
2. Toss with vinegar, pickles, eggs, bell pepper and salt.
3. Whisk together mayonnaise, scallions, celery, mustard, pickle juice and sugar.
4. Salt to taste.
5. Pour over the potatoes.
6. Gently stir to combine.
7. Chill if desired.
8. Serve and enjoy!

# Sweet Relish Potato Salad

## Ingredients:

2 pounds russet potatoes
2 tbsps. white wine vinegar
1/2 tsp. salt.
Mix
1 cup whipped salad dressing (such as Miracle Whip)
1/2 cup relish
2 tbsps. yellow mustard
1 chopped scallion

## Directions:

1. Boil, peel and cube the potatoes.
2. In a large bowl, toss together potatoes with vinegar and salt.
3. In a medium bowl, whisk together salad dressing, relish, mustard and scallion.
4. Pour over the potatoes.
5. Gently stir to combine.
6. Chill if desired.
7. Serve and enjoy!

# Crab Boil Potato Salad

## Ingredients:

2 pounds red potatoes, boiled and cubed
1/2 cup corn
1/2 cup celery, chopped
1 cup mayonnaise
1 tbsp. lemon juice
1 1/2 tsps. Old Bay
1 cup crabmeat

## Directions:

1. Boil, peel and cube the potatoes.
2. In a large bowl, toss together potatoes, celery, corn and crabmeat.
3. In a medium bowl, whisk together mayonnaise, lemon juice and Old Bay.
4. Pour over the potato mixture.
5. Gently stir to combine.
6. Chill if desired.
7. Serve and enjoy!

# Lobster Potato Salad

## Ingredients:

1 pound red potatoes, boiled and cubed
1/4 cup mayonnaise
1/4 cup creme fraiche
2 tsps. truffle oil
2 tsps. tarragon, chopped
Salt to taste
1 cup lobster meat.

## Directions:

1. Boil, peel and cube the potatoes.
2. In a large bowl, toss together potatoes and lobster.
3. In a medium bowl, whisk together mayonnaise, creme fraiche, truffle oil, tarragon, and salt.
4. Pour over the potato mixture.
5. Gently stir to combine.
6. Chill if desired.
7. Serve and enjoy!

# Curry Potato Salad

## Ingredients:

2 pounds russet potatoes, boiled, cubed
1/3 cup golden raisins
1/3 cup olive oil
2 tsps. curry powder
1 cup Greek yogurt
2 cups cooked green beans
Salt to taste

## Directions:

1. Heat olive oil and raisins in a skillet.
2. Add curry powder and stir 30 seconds.
3. Remove from heat and add Greek yogurt.
4. Boil, peel and cube the potatoes.
5. In a large bowl, toss together potatoes and green beans.
6. Pour raisin mixture over the potato mixture.
7. Gently stir to combine.
8. Season with salt.
9. Serve and enjoy!

# Ranch Potato Salad

## Ingredients:

2 pounds red potatoes, boiled, cubed
2/3 cup mayonnaise
1/4 cup buttermilk
2 tbsps. cider vinegar
1 minced garlic clove
1/2 cup chopped celery
2 chopped scallions
1 tsp. sugar
Salt and pepper to taste

## Directions:

1. Boil, peel and cube the potatoes.
2. In a large bowl, toss together potatoes and celery.
3. In a medium bowl, whisk together mayonnaise, buttermilk, vinegar, garlic, scallions, sugar, and salt and pepper.
4. Pour over the potato mixture.
5. Gently stir to combine.
6. Chill if desired.
7. Serve and enjoy!

# Bacon Ranch Potato Salad

## Ingredients:

2 pounds red potatoes, boiled, cubed
6 slices bacon
2/3 cup mayonnaise
1/4 cup buttermilk
2 tbsps. cider vinegar
1 minced garlic clove
1/2 cup chopped celery
2 chopped scallions
1 tsp. sugar
Salt and pepper to taste

## Directions:

1. Boil, peel and cube the potatoes.
2. Cook bacon until crisp.
3. Drain on paper towels.
4. In a large bowl, toss together potatoes and celery.
5. In a medium bowl, whisk together mayonnaise, buttermilk, vinegar, garlic, scallions, sugar, and salt and pepper.
6. Pour over the potato mixture.
7. Gently stir to combine.
8. Crumble bacon and add to potatoes.
9. Gently stir in bacon.
10. Chill if desired.
11. Serve and enjoy!

# Chipotle Ranch Potato Salad

## Ingredients:

2 pounds red potatoes, boiled, cubed
2/3 cup mayonnaise
1/4 cup buttermilk
2 tbsps. cider vinegar
1 minced garlic clove
1/2 cup chopped celery
2 chopped scallions
1 tsp. sugar
Salt and pepper to taste
2 tbsps. chipotle hot sauce
2 tsps. orange zest
1/4 cup chopped cilantro

## Directions:

1. Boil, peel and cube the potatoes.
2. In a large bowl, toss together potatoes and celery.
3. In a medium bowl, whisk together mayonnaise, buttermilk, chipotle hot sauce, vinegar, garlic, scallions, sugar, orange zest, cilantro and salt and pepper.
4. Pour over the potato mixture.
5. Gently stir to combine.
6. Chill if desired.
7. Serve and enjoy!

# Garden Potato Salad

## Ingredients:

2 pounds red potatoes
1 sliced carrot
1 cup sliced radishes
1 chopped cucumber,
3 chopped scallions
1/4 cup parsley, chopped
1/4 cup chives, chopped
Mix 1/2 cup mayonnaise
1/4 cup white wine vinegar
Salt and pepper to taste

## Directions:

1. Peel, cube and boil the potatoes.
2. Add carrots during the last minute of boiling.
3. Drain.
4. In a large bowl, toss together with radishes, cucumber, scallions
5. In a medium bowl, whisk together mayonnaise, vinegar, salt and pepper.
6. Pour over potato mixture.
7. Gently stir to combine.
8. Chill if desired.
9. Serve and enjoy!

# Ham and Cheese Potato Salad

## Ingredients:

2 pounds Yukon gold potatoes, boiled, cubed
1 cup mayonnaise
2 tbsps. mustard
8 oz. cubed ham
6 oz. shredded cheddar
1/2 cup red onion, diced
1/2 cup pickles, diced
2 tbsps. pickled green chiles, chopped

## Directions:

1. Boil, peel and cube the potatoes.
2. In a large bowl, toss together potatoes, ham, cheddar, onion and pickles, and chiles.
3. In a medium bowl, whisk together mayonnaise, mustard, ham, cheddar, onion, pickles, and chiles.
4. Pour over potato mixture.
5. Gently stir to combine.
6. Chill if desired.
7. Serve and enjoy!

# Green Goddess Potato Salad

## Ingredients:

2 pounds boiled, fingerling potatoes, halved
1 cup mayonnaise
1/4 cup parsley, tarragon and basil, mixed
1 scallion, diced
1 tsp. sugar
1 dash lemon juice
Salt to taste

## Directions:

1. Half and boil the potatoes.
2. In a medium bowl, whisk together mayonnaise, parsley, tarragon, basil, scallion, sugar, lemon juice and salt.
3. Pour over potatoes.
4. Gently stir to combine.
5. Chill if desired.
6. Serve and enjoy!

# Avocado Shrimp Potato Salad

## Ingredients:

2 pounds boiled, fingerling potatoes, halved
1 cup mayonnaise
1/4 cup parsley, tarragon and basil, mixed
1 scallion, diced
1 tsp. sugar
1 dash lemon juice
Salt to taste
Avocado, diced
Cooked shrimp

## Directions:

1. Half and boil the potatoes.
2. In a medium bowl, whisk together mayonnaise, parsley, tarragon, basil, scallion, sugar, lemon juice and salt.
3. Pour over potatoes.
4. Gently stir to combine.
5. Chill if desired.
6. Top with shrimp and avocado.
7. Serve and enjoy!

# Coleslaw Potato Salad

## Ingredients:

2 pounds new potatoes, boiled and quartered
1/3 cup mayonnaise
1/3 cup olive oil
1/4 cup whole grain mustard
salt and pepper
3 cups coleslaw mix
3 scallions, chopped

## Directions:

1. Boil, peel and quarter the potatoes.
2. In a large bowl, toss together coleslaw mix, scallions and potatoes.
3. In a medium bowl, whisk together mayonnaise, olive oil, mustard, salt and pepper.
4. Pour over potato mixture.
5. Gently stir to combine.
6. Chill if desired.
7. Top with shrimp and avocado.
8. Serve and enjoy!

# Dill Potato Salad

## Ingredients:

2 pounds russet potatoes, boiled, cubed
1/2 cup mayonnaise
1/2 cup sour cream
1/4 cup dill, diced
1/4 cup scallions, diced
1 tsp. sugar
2 tbsps. cider vinegar
Salt to taste

## Directions:

1. Boil, peel and cube the potatoes.
2. Put the potatoes in a large bowl.
3. In a medium bowl, whisk together sour cream, mayonnaise, dill, scallions, sugar, vinegar, and salt.
4. Pour over potatoes.
5. Gently stir to combine.
6. Chill if desired.
7. Serve and enjoy!

# Beet Dill Potato Salad

## Ingredients:

2 pounds russet potatoes, boiled, cubed
1/2 cup mayonnaise
1/2 cup sour cream
1/4 cup dill, diced
1/4 cup scallions, diced
1 tsp. sugar
2 tbsps. cider vinegar
1 cup roasted beets, sliced
Salt to taste

## Directions:

1. Boil, peel and cube the potatoes.
2. Put the potatoes in a large bowl and toss with beets.
3. In a medium bowl, whisk together sour cream, mayonnaise, dill, scallions, sugar, vinegar, and salt.
4. Pour over potatoes and beets.
5. Gently stir to combine.
6. Chill if desired.
7. Serve and enjoy!

# Nordic Potato Salad

## Ingredients:

2 pounds russet potatoes, boiled, cubed
1/2 cup mayonnaise
1/2 cup sour cream
1/4 cup dill, diced
1/4 cup scallions, diced
1 tsp. sugar
2 tbsps. cider vinegar
1 cup roasted beets, sliced
2 tbsps. horseradish
Salt to taste

## Directions:

1. Boil, peel and cube the potatoes.
2. Put the potatoes in a large bowl and toss with beets.
3. In a medium bowl, whisk together sour cream, mayonnaise, horseradish, dill, scallions, sugar, vinegar, and salt.
4. Pour over potatoes and beets.
5. Gently stir to combine.
6. Chill if desired.
7. Serve and enjoy!

# Dutch Potato Salad

## Ingredients:

2 pounds russet potatoes, boiled, cubed
1/2 cup sour cream
3/4 cup mayonnaise
2 tbsps. horseradish
2 tbsps. cider vinegar
2 tsps. caraway seeds
1 tsp. sugar
2 chopped cucumbers
4 chopped scallions
2 pounds boiled, cubed russets

## Directions:

1. Boil, peel and cube the potatoes.
2. In a large bowl, toss together potatoes cucumbers and scallions.
3. In a medium bowl, whisk together sour cream, mayonnaise, horseradish, cider vinegar, caraway seeds and sugar.
4. Pour over potato mixture.
5. Gently stir to combine.
6. Chill if desired.
7. Serve and enjoy!

# Peruvian Potato Salad

## Ingredients:

2 pounds Yukon gold potatoes, boiled and cubed
1/2 cup evaporated milk
1/3 cup queso fresco
1 tbsp. aji amarillo paste
1 tbsp. vegetable oil
1/4 cup olives, chopped
2 hard boiled eggs, sliced

## Directions:

1. Boil, peel and cube the potatoes.
2. In a large bowl, toss together potatoes and olives.
3. In a medium bowl, whisk together evaporated milk, queso fresco, aji amarillo paste and vegetable oil.
4. Pour over potato mixture.
5. Gently stir to combine.
6. Top with sliced eggs.
7. Chill if desired.
8. Serve and enjoy!

# Chicken Potato Salad

## Ingredients:

1 1/2 cups grilled chicken, diced
2 pounds fingerling potatoes, boiled and halved
1 1/2 tbsps. champagne vinegar
1 1/2 tbsps. Dijon mustard
1/3 cup olive oil
1/4 cup chopped cornichons
Parsley, chopped
Salt and pepper to taste

## Directions:

1. Boil, peel and cube the potatoes.
2. In a large bowl, toss together potatoes, cornichons, parsley.
3. In a medium bowl, whisk together vinegar and mustard, olive oil and salt and pepper.
4. Pour over potato mixture.
5. Gently stir to combine.
6. Top with sliced eggs.
7. Chill if desired.
8. Serve and enjoy!

# Herb Vinegar Potato Salad

## Ingredients:

2 pounds new potatoes, boiled and quartered
1 cup mixed chopped parsley, dill and chives
1/2 cup shallots, chopped
6 tbsps. white wine vinegar
6 tbsps. olive oil
Salt and pepper to taste

## Directions:

1. Boil and quarter the potatoes.
2. In a large bowl, toss together potatoes, cornichons and parsley.
3. In a medium bowl, whisk together parsley, dill and chives, shallots, vinegar and olive oil, salt and pepper.
4. Pour over potatoes.
5. Gently stir to combine.
6. Top with sliced eggs.
7. Chill if desired.
8. Serve and enjoy!

# Tomato Potato Salad

## Ingredients:

2 pounds new potatoes, boiled and quartered
1 cup mixed chopped parsley, dill and chives
1/2 cup shallots, chopped
6 tbsps. white wine vinegar
6 tbsps. olive oil
1/2 cup red onion, sliced
2 cups grape tomatoes, halved
Salt and pepper to taste

## Directions:

1. Boil and quarter the potatoes.
2. Soak sliced red onion in ice water for 1/2 hour, then drain.
3. In a large bowl, toss together potatoes, cornichons, tomatoes, onion and parsley.
4. In a medium bowl, whisk together parsley, dill and chives, shallots, vinegar and olive oil, salt and pepper.
5. Pour over potatoes.
6. Gently stir to combine.
7. Top with sliced eggs.
8. Chill if desired.
9. Serve and enjoy!

# French Potato Salad

## Ingredients:
2 pounds fingerling potatoes, boiled and halved
1 cup chopped mixed parsley, chives and tarragon
1/2 cup shallot, chopped
1/3 cup white wine
1/4 cup olive oil
2 tbsps. white wine vinegar
2 tbsps. Dijon mustard
Salt and pepper to taste

## Directions:
1. Boil and half the potatoes.
2. Put potatoes in a large bowl.
3. In a medium bowl, whisk together parsley, chives, tarragon, shallots, wine, olive oil, vinegar, mustard, salt and pepper.
4. Pour over potatoes.
5. Gently stir to combine.
6. Chill if desired.
7. Serve and enjoy!

# Niçoise Potato Salad

## Ingredients:

2 pounds fingerling potatoes, boiled and halved
1 cup chopped mixed parsley, chives and tarragon
1/2 cup shallot, chopped
2 cups green beans, chopped
1/3 cup white wine
1/4 cup olive oil
2 tbsps. white wine vinegar
2 tbsps. Dijon mustard
1 can oil-packed tuna, drained
1/2 cup Kalamata olives, halved
Salt and pepper to taste

## Directions:

1. Boil and half the potatoes.
2. Add the green beans to the potatoes during the last four minutes of cooking.
3. In a large bowl, toss together potatoes, green beans, olives and tuna.
4. In a medium bowl, whisk together parsley, chives, tarragon, shallots, wine, olive oil, vinegar, mustard, salt and pepper.
5. Pour over potatoes.
6. Gently stir to combine.
7. Chill if desired.
8. Serve and enjoy!

# Provençal Potato Salad

## Ingredients:

2 pounds fingerling potatoes, boiled and halved
1 cup chopped mixed parsley, chives and tarragon
1/2 cup shallot, chopped
1/3 cup white wine
1/4 cup olive oil
2 tbsps. white wine vinegar
2 tbsps. Dijon mustard
2 cups grape tomatoes, halved
1 fennel bulb, shaved
1/2 cup Kalamata olives, halved
Fennel fronds, chopped
Salt and pepper to taste

## Directions:

1. Boil and half the potatoes.
2. Put potatoes in a large bowl.
3. Toss potatoes with tomatoes, fennel, olives and fronds.
4. In a medium bowl, whisk together parsley, chives, tarragon, shallots, wine, olive oil, vinegar, mustard, salt and pepper.
5. Pour over potato mixture.
6. Gently stir to combine.
7. Chill if desired.
8. Serve and enjoy!

# Pesto Pea Potato Salad

## Ingredients:

2 pounds Yukon gold potatoes, peeled and cubed
1 cup frozen peas
6 tbsps. white wine vinegar
1/4 cup pesto
Pine nuts
Salt and pepper to taste

## Directions:

1. Boil and cube the potatoes.
2. Add peas during the last 4 minutes of cooking.
3. Drain.
4. Add potatoes and peas to a large bowl.
5. In a medium bowl, whisk together vinegar, pesto, Salt and pepper.
6. Pour over potato mixture.
7. Gently stir to combine.
8. Add pine nuts.
9. Stir again.
10. Chill if desired.
11. Serve and enjoy!

# Patriotic Potato Salad

## Ingredients:

2 pounds mixed red, white and purple potatoes, cubed
4 tbsps. cider vinegar, divided
1/2 cup celery, diced
1/4 cup scallions, diced
1/4 cup olive oil
2 tbsps. whole grain mustard
salt and pepper to taste

## Directions:

1. Boil and cube potatoes with 2 tbsps. cider vinegar.
2. Drain and put in a large bowl.
3. Add celery and scallions and gently toss.
4. Whisk together olive oil, 2 tbsps. vinegar, mustard, salt and pepper.
5. Pour over potato mixture.
6. Gently stir to combine.
7. Stir again.
8. Chill if desired.
9. Serve and enjoy!

# Pico de Gallo Potato Salad

## Ingredients:

2 pounds Yukon Gold potatoes, boiled and cubed
2 tbsps. olive oil
1 tbsp. cider vinegar
3 cups fresh salsa
Salt to taste

## Directions:

1. Boil and cube potatoes.
2. Drain and put in a large bowl.
3. Add celery and olive oil, vinegar, salsa and salt.
4. Gently stir to combine.
5. Chill if desired.
6. Serve and enjoy!

# Salsa Verde Potato Salad

## Ingredients:

2 pounds Yukon Gold potatoes, boiled and cubed
1 cup red onion, sliced
1 cup bell pepper, sliced
1 1/2 cups salsa verde
1 avocado, chopped
Salt to taste
Cilantro
Cotija cheese

## Directions:

1. Boil and cube potatoes.
2. Drain and put in a large bowl.
3. Add onion, bell pepper, salsa verde, avocado and salt.
4. Gently stir to combine.
5. Top with cilantro and cotija cheese.
6. Chill if desired.
7. Serve and enjoy!

# Sichuan Potato Salad

## Ingredients:

2 russet potatoes, cut into matchsticks
2 sliced garlic cloves
1 tsp. sugar
1 tsp. salt
2 dried red chiles
Peanut oil
3 chopped scallions
1 1/2 tsps. balsamic vinegar
1 tsp. sesame oil

## Directions:

1. Cut 2 russets into matchsticks.
2. Boil 1 minute.
3. Cook garlic, sugar, salt and chiles in a skillet with peanut oil, 30 seconds.
4. Add scallions.
5. Drain the potatoes and toss with the flavored oil, vinegar and sesame oil.
6. Chill if desired.
7. Serve and enjoy!

# Carrot Sesame Potato Salad

## Ingredients:

2 pounds red potatoes, sliced
4 carrots, matchstick cut
4 scallions, diced
1/2 cup bottled sesame-ginger dressing
Sesame seeds

## Directions:

1. Boil potatoes, add carrots during the last 2 minutes.
2. Drain and toss with scallions and dressing.
3. Top with sesame seeds.
4. Chill if desired.
5. Serve and enjoy!

# Salt Cod Potato Salad

## Ingredients:

1 pound Yukon Gold potatoes, boiled cubed
3 sliced garlic cloves
1/4 cup olive oil
3/4 cup tomato, diced
1/2 cup salt cod, flaked
Parsley, diced

## Directions:

1. Cook garlic cloves in a skillet with olive oil until soft.
2. Mix with tomato, cod and potatoes.
3. Top with chopped parsley.
4. Serve and enjoy!

# Thai Potato Salad

## Ingredients:

2 pounds russet potatoes, boiled and cubed
1/3 cup mayonnaise
1/3 cup unsweetened coconut milk
1 tbsp. curry paste
1 tbsp. lime juice
Salt to taste
1 bell pepper, diced
Basil, diced
Mint, diced

## Directions:

1. Boil and cube potatoes.
2. Drain and put in a large bowl.
3. Add bell pepper, basil and mint.
4. Gently toss.
5. In a medium bowl, whisk together mayonnaise coconut milk, curry paste, lime juice, and salt.
6. Pour over potato mixture.
7. Gently stir to combine.
8. Stir again.
9. Chill if desired.
10. Serve and enjoy!

# Indian Potato Salad

## Ingredients:

2 pounds russet potatoes, boiled and cubed
1 tbsp. garam masala
1 tbsp. grated ginger
1 tbsp. canola oil
1 cup Greek yogurt
1/2 cup mayonnaise
1 cup chickpeas
Salt and pepper to taste
Cilantro

## Directions:

1. Boil and cube potatoes.
2. Drain and put in a large bowl.
3. Add chickpeas and gently toss.
4. Cook garam masala, ginger and canola oil in a skillet for 30 seconds.
5. Mix with Greek yogurt and mayonnaise in a medium bowl.
6. Pour over potato mixture.
7. Gently mix to combine
8. Season with salt and pepper.
9. Top with cilantro.
10. Serve and enjoy!

# Greek Potato Salad

## Ingredients:

1 cup Greek yogurt
1/4 cup olive oil
Salt and pepper to taste
2 pounds Yukon gold potatoes, boiled and cubed
1 cup chopped cucumber
1/2 cup crumbled feta
3 tbsps. red onion, diced
3 tbsps. mint, diced
Oregano

## Directions:

1. Boil and cube potatoes.
2. Drain and put in a large bowl.
3. Add cucumber, feta, onion, mint, and oregano.
4. Gently toss to combine.
5. In a medium bowl, whisk together Greek yogurt, olive oil, salt and pepper.
6. Pour over potato mixture.
7. Gently mix to combine
8. Chill if desired.
9. Serve and enjoy!

# Caviar Potato Salad

## Ingredients:

2 pounds new potatoes, boiled and halved
1/2 cup creme fraiche
2 tbsps. white wine vinegar
2 tbsps. olive oil
2 tbsps. red onion, minced
1 tbsp. Dijon mustard
Chives, minced
chervil, minced
Salt and pepper to taste
Salmon caviar

## Directions:

1. Boil and half the potatoes.
2. Drain and put in a large bowl.
3. In a medium bowl, whisk together creme fraiche, vinegar, olive oil, onion, mustard, chives, chervil, and salt and pepper.
4. Pour over potatoes.
5. Gently toss to combine.
6. Top with caviar.

# Amish Potato Salad

## Ingredients:

3 lbs. potatoes, cut into quarters
3/4 cup mayonnaise
3/4 cup sugar
2 tbsp. yellow mustard
2 tbsp. vinegar
1 1/2 tsp. salt
4 hard boiled eggs, peeled and chopped
1/2 cup onions, finely chopped
2 stalks celery, chopped

## Directions:

1. Place the potatoes in a large pot, fill with enough water to cover potatoes.
2. Bring to a boil and cook about 20 minutes, or until fork tender.
3. Drain, set aside to cool.
4. In a medium bowl combine mayo, sugar, mustard, vinegar and salt, mix well.
5. Place the potatoes, eggs, onion and celery in a large bowl.
6. Pour in the dressing and gently stir until thoroughly mixed. Chill 2 to 3 hours before serving.

# Honey Mustard Potato Salad

## Ingredients:

2 lbs. Idaho potatoes with skin on, cut into 1-1/2-inch chunks
1 cup mayonnaise
1/8 cup honey
1 tbsp. prepared mustard
1/4 tsp. salt
1/4 cup sliced scallions (1 to 2 scallions)
3 slices cooked bacon, crumbled

## Directions:

1. In a large pot of boiling, salted water, cook potatoes 15 to 20 minutes, or until fork tender.
2. Place in a large bowl and set aside.
3. In a small bowl, combine mayonnaise, honey, mustard, and salt.
4. Mix well.
5. Gently toss dressing with potatoes until well coated.
6. Add scallions and bacon and toss gently; chill until ready to serve.

# Classic American Style Potato Salad

## Ingredients:
2 pounds red boiling potatoes, scrubbed
2 tbsps. red wine vinegar
1/2 tsp. salt
1/2 tsp. freshly ground black pepper
3 hard-cooked eggs
1 small celery stalk
1/4 cup chopped sweet pickle (not relish)
3 scallions
2 tbsp. chopped fresh parsley
1/2 cup mayonnaise
2 tbsps. Dijon-style mustard

## Directions:
1. Place potatoes in a pot with water to cover.
2. Bring to a boil, cover and simmer, stirring to ensure even cooking, until a thin-bladed paring knife or a metal skewer inserted into a potato can be removed with no resistance, 25 to 30 minutes.
3. Drain, rinse under cold water and drain again.
4. Cool slightly.
5. Cut warm potatoes into 3/4-inch dice with a serrated knife.
6. Layer them in a bowl, seasoning with vinegar, salt and pepper as you go.
7. Cut eggs, celery and pickle in 1/4-inch dice and thinly slice scallions.
8. Add to potatoes, along with parsley.
9. Stir in mayonnaise and mustard until everything is combined.
10. Chill, covered, before serving.
11. Serve and enjoy!

# Garden Potato Salad

Ingredients
3 pounds new potatoes, halved
1 1/2 tsps. kosher salt, divided
4 oz. fresh snow peas or sugar snap peas
3 tbsps. coarse-grained Dijon mustard
3 tbsps. fresh lemon juice
1 tsp. sugar
1/4 tsp. freshly ground black pepper
2/3 cup olive oil
1 cup loosely packed fresh herbs (such as basil, chives, mint, and dill), coarsely chopped

## Directions:

1. Bring potatoes, water to cover, and 1 tsp. salt to a boil in a large Dutch oven over medium-high heat.
2. Reduce heat to medium-low, and cook 10 to 15 minutes or until tender; drain.
3. Cool 30 minutes.
4. Cook snow peas in 2 cups boiling water in a medium saucepan over medium-high heat 1 minute or until crisp-tender; drain, pressing between paper towels.
5. Cut peas into 1/2-inch pieces.
6. Cover with plastic wrap, and chill until ready to use.
7. Whisk together mustard, next 3 ingredients, and remaining 1/2 tsp. salt in a medium bowl; gradually add olive oil in a slow, steady stream, whisking until smooth.
8. Gently toss together potatoes and 1/2 cup dressing in a large bowl, and let stand 30 minutes.
9. Just before serving, gently stir in peas, herbs, and remaining dressing.
10. Add salt and pepper to taste.

# Veggie Potato Salad

## Ingredients:

2 1/2 pounds baby red potatoes, cut into 1-inch cubes
2 tbsps. apple cider vinegar
1 tbsp. olive oil
1/2 cup whole buttermilk
1/4 cup reduced-fat sour cream
1/4 cup reduced-fat mayonnaise with olive oil
1 tbsp. Dijon mustard
2 carrots, grated
1/2 cup chopped celery
1/2 cup sliced radishes
1/2 cup steamed, cut fresh green beans
1/4 cup finely chopped fresh parsley
1 tbsp. lemon zest
1 garlic clove, minced
Sea salt
Freshly ground pepper to taste

## Directions:

1. Bring potatoes and salted water to cover to a boil in a large saucepan; reduce heat, and simmer 7 to 10 minutes or until tender.
2. Drain.
3. Place potatoes in a large bowl; sprinkle with vinegar and oil, and toss gently.
4. Cool completely (about 1 hour).
5. Whisk together buttermilk and next 3 ingredients.
6. Stir in carrots and next 6 ingredients.
7. Season with salt and pepper to taste. Spoon buttermilk mixture over potato mixture; toss gently to coat.
8. Cover and chill 1 to 24 hours before serving.

# Blue Cheese and Bacon Potato Salad

## Ingredients:

3 pounds baby red potatoes, cut in half
2 tbsps. olive oil
1 tsp. salt
1 tsp. freshly ground pepper
1 cup mayonnaise
1/4 cup chopped fresh parsley
1/4 cup white balsamic vinegar*
2 tsps. sugar
2 tsps. Dijon mustard
1 cup thinly sliced red onion
4 oz. crumbled blue cheese
6 bacon slices, cooked and crumbled

## Directions:

1. Preheat grill to 350 degrees to 400 degrees F (medium-high) heat.
2. Place potatoes in a single layer in center of a large piece of heavy-duty aluminum foil. Drizzle with olive oil; sprinkle with salt and pepper.
3. Bring up foil sides over potatoes; double fold top and side edges to seal, making 1 large packet.
4. Grill potatoes, in foil packet, covered with grill lid, 15 minutes on each side.
5. Remove packet from grill.
6. Carefully open packet, using tongs, and let potatoes cool 5 minutes.
7. Whisk together mayonnaise and next 4 ingredients in a large bowl; add potatoes, tossing gently to coat.
8. Stir in onion, blue cheese, and bacon.

# Dill Potato Salad

## Ingredients:

2 pounds small red potatoes, unpeeled
1/3 cup red wine vinegar
1/3 cup vegetable oil
3 tbsps. chopped fresh or 1 tbsp. dried dill
1/2 to 1 tsp. salt
1/2 tsp. pepper
1 large red bell pepper, chopped
1 cucumber, cut in half lengthwise and sliced
1/2 cup sliced green onions
1 (4 oz.) package crumbled feta cheese

## Directions:

1. Bring potatoes and water to cover to a boil.
2. Cook 25 to 30 minutes or just until tender; drain and cool.
3. Cut potatoes into quarters.
4. Whisk together vinegar, oil, dill, salt, and pepper.
5. Pour over warm potatoes.
6. Stir in chopped bell pepper, cucumber, and green onions; add cheese, and toss to combine.
7. Cover and chill at least 2 hours.

# Italian Potato Salad

## Ingredients:

2 pounds fingerling potatoes
3 (4-inch) fresh rosemary sprigs
2 garlic cloves
2 bay leaves
1/4 cup olive oil
2 tsps. kosher salt
1 (2-oz.) salami piece, cut into thin strips
2 tbsps. chopped shallot (1/2 large shallot)
3 tbsps. sherry or red wine vinegar
1 tbsp. Dijon mustard
2 tsps. sorghum syrup or honey
1/4 tsp. dried crushed red pepper
1/3 cup olive oil
2 cups loosely packed baby arugula
1 tbsp. chopped fresh tarragon or basil

## Directions:

1. Bring first 5 ingredients and water to cover to a boil in a Dutch oven over medium-high heat, and boil 15 to 20 minutes or until potatoes are tender.
2. Drain; discard rosemary, garlic, and bay leaves.
3. Sprinkle potatoes with salt; gently stir to coat.
4. Cool 10 minutes.
5. Meanwhile, sauté salami in a medium-size nonstick skillet over medium heat 1 to 2 minutes or until crisp; drain on paper towels.
6. Whisk together shallot and next 4 ingredients.
7. Add 1/3 cup olive oil in a slow, steady stream, whisking constantly until smooth.
8. Cut potatoes in half lengthwise.
9. Toss together potatoes, vinegar mixture, arugula, and tarragon.
10. Add salt and pepper to taste.
11. Top with salami just before serving.

# Roasted New Potato Salad

## Ingredients:

2 tbsps. olive oil
2 pounds small red potatoes, diced
1/2 medium-size sweet onion, chopped
2 tsps. minced garlic
1 tsp. coarse salt
1/2 tsp. freshly ground pepper
8 to 10 cooked crisp bacon slices, crumbled
1 bunch green onions, chopped
3/4 cup prepared Ranch dressing
Salt and pepper to taste

## Directions:

1. Place oil in a 15- x 10-inch jellyroll pan.
2. Add potatoes and the next 4 ingredients, tossing to coat.
3. Arrange potato mixture in a single layer.
4. Bake at 425° for 30 to 35 minutes or until potatoes are tender, stirring occasionally.
5. Transfer to a large bowl.
6. Toss together potatoes, bacon, green onions, and dressing.
7. Add salt and pepper to taste.
8. Serve immediately or cover and chill until ready to serve.

# Herbed Potato Salad

2 pounds red potatoes, cubed
1 (14-oz.) can fat-free chicken broth
1 garlic clove, minced
1/2 cup nonfat plain yogurt
1 tbsp. chopped fresh dill
1 tbsp. chopped fresh oregano
2 tbsps. light mayonnaise
2 tbsps. olive oil
2 tbsps. white wine vinegar
1 tsp. salt

## Directions:

1. Bring first 3 ingredients and 2 cups water to a boil in a large saucepan over medium-high heat, and cook 20 minutes or until tender.
2. Drain and let cool 30 minutes.
3. Whisk together yogurt and next 6 ingredients in a large bowl until combined.
4. Gently fold potatoes into yogurt mixture.
5. Cover and chill 1 to 12 hours.

# Lemon Potato Salad

## Ingredients:

2 pounds red potatoes, cut into eighths
1/4 cup olive oil
3 tbsps. lemon juice
3/4 tsp. salt
1/2 tsp. dry mustard
1/4 tsp. freshly ground pepper
3 green onions, thinly sliced
2 tbsps. chopped fresh parsley

## Directions:

1. Bring potatoes and salted cold water to cover to a boil in a large Dutch oven.
2. Boil 15 to 17 minutes or just until tender.
3. Drain and let cool 5 minutes.
4. Whisk together olive oil and next 4 ingredients in a large bowl.
5. Add warm potatoes, green onions, and parsley; toss to coat.
6. Serve at room temperature or chilled.

# Spanish Potato Salad

## Ingredients:

1 pound small red potatoes
3 tbsps. olive oil
1 tbsp. red wine vinegar
2 garlic cloves, crushed
1 small red bell pepper, chopped
2 tbsps. pimento-stuffed green olives, sliced
1 tbsp. minced shallot 1 tbsp. chopped fresh parsley salt and ground black pepper to taste 1 lemon, cut into wedges (optional)

## Directions:

1. Place potatoes into a pot and cover with salted water; bring to a boil.
2. Reduce heat to medium-low and simmer until tender, about 10 minutes.
3. Drain and cool until easily handled.
4. Slice potatoes about 1/2-inch thick and place in a bowl.
5. Whisk olive oil and vinegar together in a bowl; stir in garlic.
6. Pour dressing over potatoes and lightly toss to coat.
7. Mix red bell pepper, green olives, shallot, parsley, salt, and pepper into potatoes.
8. Serve salad with lemon wedges to squeeze over each serving.

# Ranch Potato Salad

## Ingredients:

5 pounds red potatoes
1 (.7 oz.) package dry Italian salad dressing mix
1/4 cup tarragon vinegar 1/4 cup water
1 cup extra-virgin olive oil 1/2 cup chopped celery
1 cup real bacon bits 1/4 cup chopped dill pickle (optional)
1/4 cup chopped green onion 3 cups mayonnaise

## Directions:

1. Place the potatoes into a large pot and cover with water.
2. Bring to a boil over high heat, then reduce heat to medium-low, cover, and simmer until tender, about 20 minutes.
3. Drain and allow to steam dry for a minute or two.
4. In a bowl, whisk together the dry Italian dressing mix, tarragon vinegar, water, and olive oil until thoroughly blended.
5. Set aside.
6. Place the hot potatoes into a large bowl, and roughly but thoroughly slice them with a table knife until the potatoes are in chunks.
7. Pour the dressing mixture over the hot potatoes, toss to coat, and let the potatoes cool.
8. Add the celery, bacon bits, dill pickle, and green onion to the potatoes; lightly stir in mayonnaise until all ingredients are well combined, and serve.

# Red Potato Salad

## Ingredients:

3 pounds red potatoes, cut into chunks
1 cup sour cream
1/2 cup mayonnaise
2 tsps. Dijon mustard 1 tsp. white vinegar
4 hard-cooked eggs, chopped 1 dill pickle, chopped
1/3 celery stalk, chopped 2 green onions, chopped
1 dash hot sauce 1 tbsp. dried dill weed
1/2 tsp. garlic powder 1 dash onion salt salt and pepper to taste

## Directions:

1. Place the potatoes in a pot with enough water to cover.
2. Bring to a boil, and cook for about 10 minutes, or until easily pierced with a fork.
3. Drain, and transfer to a large bowl to cool.
4. In a medium bowl, mix the sour cream, mayonnaise, mustard, vinegar, eggs, pickle, celery, green onions, and hot sauce.
5. Season with dill, garlic powder, onion salt, salt, and pepper.
6. Pour over the potatoes, and gently toss to coat. Chill at least 3 hours in the refrigerator before serving.

# Oktoberfest Potato Salad

## Ingredients:

6 potatoes
1 tsp. dry mustard powder
1 tsp. water
4 slices bacon
1/4 cup chopped onion
1/4 cup white sugar
1/4 cup water
1/2 cup cider vinegar
1 cup diced celery, divided
3 tbsps. chopped fresh parsley, divided
Salt and ground black pepper to taste

## Directions:

1. Place potatoes into a large pot and cover with salted water; bring to a boil.
2. Reduce heat to medium-low and simmer until tender, about 20 minutes.
3. Drain and let cool.
4. Mix dry mustard with 1 tsp. water in a small bowl and let stand 10 minutes to develop flavor.
5. Place bacon in a large skillet and cook over medium-high heat, turning occasionally, until evenly browned, about 10 minutes.
6. Drain the bacon slices on paper towels. Reserve bacon drippings in skillet.
7. Let bacon cool; crumble bacon.
8. Cook onion in reserved bacon drippings over medium heat until onion is translucent and soft, about 5 minutes.
9. Stir mustard paste, sugar, 1/4 cup water, and cider vinegar into onion; bring to a boil.
10. Reduce heat to low and simmer vinegar dressing for 2 minutes.
11. Peel potatoes if desired; slice 3 potatoes into a salad bow and arrange into a layer.

12. Sprinkle potatoes with half the crumbled bacon, celery, and parsley; season with salt and black pepper.
13. Pour a little of the vinegar dressing over the layer.
14. Repeat layer with remaining 3 potatoes, bacon, celery, parsley, salt, and black pepper; pour remaining dressing over the salad.
15. Cover and let stand at room temperature for 30 minutes before serving.

# Canadian Potato Salad

## Ingredients:

4 pounds russet potatoes
3 tbsps. cider vinegar
3 large eggs
2/3 cup mayonnaise, or more to taste
2 tsps. salt
1 tsp. dry mustard
1/2 tsp. celery seed
1/2 tsp. ground black pepper
2 tbsps. hot water, or as needed
3 stalks celery, diced
1 red bell pepper, seeded and diced
1 onion, finely diced
3 green onions, thinly sliced
1/4 cup diced dill pickles
2 tbsps. chopped fresh parsley
1 tsp. paprika

## Directions:

1. Place potatoes in a large pot and cover with salted water; bring to a boil.
2. Reduce heat to medium-low; simmer until tender, about 25 minutes.
3. Drain.
4. Cut potatoes into 1-inch cubes, leaving skin on.
5. Drizzle potatoes with vinegar while warm; set aside to cool completely, about 20 minutes.
6. Place eggs in a saucepan, cover with water, and bring to a boil.
7. Remove from heat; let eggs stand in hot water for 15 minutes.
8. Remove eggs from hot water; cool under cold running water.
9. Peel eggs; cut 2 eggs into 1/4-inch dice.

10. Slice the remaining egg into 1/4-inch slices; set aside for garnish.
11. Stir together the 2 diced eggs, mayonnaise, salt, dry mustard, celery seed, and black pepper in a large bowl; stir in hot water.
12. Stir potatoes, celery, red bell pepper, onion, green onions, pickles, and parsley into mayonnaise mixture; cover and chill in the refrigerator for 30 minutes.
13. Sprinkle salad with paprika and arrange reserved egg slices on top before serving.

# Caribbean Potato Salad

## Ingredients:

1 large russet potato, peeled and quartered
1 large sweet potato, peeled and quartered
1 cup corn
1 tsp. prepared Dijon-style mustard
2 tbsps. fresh lime juice
3 tbsps. chopped fresh cilantro
1 clove garlic, minced
3 tbsps. canola oil
1/2 tsp. salt
1/4 tsp. ground black pepper
1 cucumber, halved lengthwise and chopped
1/2 red onion, thinly sliced
1/4 cup finely chopped peanuts

## Directions:

1. Place the Russet potato pieces into a large saucepan, and cover with salted water.
2. Bring to a boil, turn the heat down, and simmer for 10 minutes.
3. Add the sweet potato, and cook about 15 minutes more.
4. Remove a piece of each potato, and cut it in half to see if it is cooked enough. Once the potatoes are tender, add corn kernels.
5. Cook another 30 seconds.
6. Drain through a colander.
7. Fill the saucepan with cold water, and drop vegetables into water.
8. Cool for 5 minutes, and drain.
9. In a large bowl, whisk together mustard, lime juice, cilantro, and garlic. Slowly whisk in oil.
10. Mix in salt and black pepper.
11. Cut cooled potatoes into 1 inch cubes, and add to dressing along with cucumber, and red onion.
12. Toss well.

13. Serve at room temperature or chilled.
14. Toss the peanuts in just before serving.

# Buttermilk No Mayonnaise Potato Salad

## Ingredients:

3 pounds petite red or Yellow Yukon potatoes, unpeeled and quartered
Salt and freshly ground black pepper
1/4 cup buttermilk
1/3 cup olive oil
2 to 3 tbsps. lemon juice, from 1 lemon
1 tbsp. honey, warmed
8 oz. tiny mozzarella balls
12 oz. cherry tomatoes, halved
2 oz. basil, roughly chopped

## Directions:

1. Heat a large pot of water to boiling and salt it generously with at least 1 tbsp. salt.
2. When the water is boiling, add the potatoes and cook for 15 to 20 minutes or until they are very tender but not yet falling apart.
3. Drain cooked potatoes and return them to the pot.
4. While the potatoes are cooking, whisk together the buttermilk, olive oil, lemon juice, honey, and 1/2 tsp. salt.
5. Pour this dressing over the warm potatoes and toss to coat.
6. Toss with the mozzarella balls, halved cherry tomatoes, and basil.
7. Season generously with salt and fresh pepper (the salad will need more salt than you expect).
8. Refrigerate for at least 1 hour before serving.
9. Serve at room temperature.

# Red No Mayo Potato Salad

## Ingredients:

4 lbs. small red potatoes, quartered
1/2 pound radishes, thinly sliced
2 bunches green onions, green parts only, thinly sliced
1/4 cup smoked olive oil
3 tbsps. ponzu
Kosher salt
Freshly ground black pepper

## Directions:

1. Heat a large pot of well-salted water over high heat.
2. When it boils, add the quartered red potatoes and cook until quite tender, about 15 to 18 minutes.
3. Drain and return to the pot.
4. Stir in the radishes, green onions, olive oil and ponzu.
5. Salt and pepper to taste.

# Southern Dill Potato Salad

## Ingredients:

10 unpeeled red potatoes
5 hard boiled eggs, roughly chopped
3/4 cup sour cream
3/4 cup mayonnaise
1 tbsp. apple cider vinegar, or to taste
1 tbsp. Dijon mustard, or to taste
1/2 white onion, finely chopped
1 stalk celery, finely chopped
1 tsp. celery salt
Salt and black pepper to taste
1 tbsp. dried dill weed

## Directions:

1. Place the potatoes in a large pot, cover them with water, and bring to a boil over high heat.
2. Reduce the heat to medium-low, and simmer until the potatoes are cooked through but still firm, about 20 minutes.
3. Remove from the water, let cool, and cut the potatoes into chunks.
4. Set the potatoes aside.
5. In a bowl, stir together the sour cream, mayonnaise, apple cider vinegar, Dijon mustard, onion, celery, celery salt, and salt and pepper until well mixed.
6. Place the potatoes and eggs in a large salad bowl, and sprinkle with dried dill.
7. Pour the dressing over the potatoes and eggs, and mix lightly.
8. Cover and refrigerate the salad for at least 30 minutes.
9. Serve and enjoy!

# Curried Potato Salad

## Ingredients:

2 lbs. red potatoes, peeled
2 eggs
1 cup mayonnaise
1 cup sour cream
2 red apples, cored and cut into 1/2 inch cubes
1/2 cup chopped red onion
1/4 cup sweet pickle relish
2 stalks celery, diced
3 green onions, thinly sliced
1 tbsp. curry powder
Salt and pepper to taste

## Directions:

1. Place the potatoes into a large pot and cover with salted water.
2. Bring to a boil over high heat, then reduce heat to medium-low, cover, and simmer until tender, about 20 minutes.
3. Drain and allow to steam dry for a minute or two.
4. Allow the potatoes to cool, then cut into chunks.
5. While the potatoes are cooking, place the eggs into a saucepan in a single layer and fill with water to cover the eggs by 1 inch.
6. Cover the saucepan and bring the water to a boil over high heat.
7. Once the water is boiling, remove from the heat and let the eggs stand in the hot water for 15 minutes.
8. Pour out the hot water, then cool the eggs under cold running water in the sink.
9. Peel and chop once cold.
10. In a large salad bowl, whisk together the mayonnaise and sour cream until smooth, then stir in the apple chunks, red onion, pickle relish, celery, green onions, curry powder, and salt and pepper.

11. Lightly stir in the potato chunks and eggs, toss to coat with dressing, cover the bowl, and chill at least 3 hours before serving.

# Maryland Potato Salad

## Ingredients:

1 large red onion, cut lengthwise and thinly sliced
1/2 cup plus
2 tbsps. cider vinegar
2 tsps. salt
5 lbs. medium yellow-fleshed potatoes such as Yukon Gold
3 tsps. Old Bay seasoning
1 1/4 tsps. sugar
3/4 cup extra-virgin olive oil

## Directions:

1. Toss onion, 2 tbsps. vinegar, and 1/2 tsp. salt in a bowl.
2. Marinate at room temperature, tossing occasionally, until slightly softened and pink, about 45 minutes.
3. Bring a large pot of salted water to a boil.
4. Add potatoes and simmer until tender, about 20-25 minutes (depending on the size of the potatoes).
5. Whisk together 3 tsps. Old Bay seasoning with sugar, remaining 11/2 tsps. salt, and remaining 1/2 cup vinegar in a small bowl.
6. Drain potatoes in a colander, and when cool enough to handle but still warm, peel and cut into bite-sized wedges.
7. Toss warm potatoes with vinegar mixture in a large bowl.
8. Add onion mixture and oil, tossing to combine.
9. Add more Old Bay seasoning, if desired (I liked mine with a couple extra tsps.).
10. Serve immediately or chill for up to 24 hours.

# Carolina Potato Salad

## Ingredients:

2 lbs. red potatoes
3 hard-cooked eggs, chopped
1/2 cup sour cream
1/2 cup mayonnaise
1/2 (4 oz.) jar chopped pimento peppers
2 green onions, chopped
2 slices cooked bacon, chopped
2 tbsps. yellow mustard
1 tbsp. white sugar
1 tbsp. red wine vinegar
1/2 tsp. salt
1/2 tsp. ground black pepper
1/2 tsp. celery seed
1/4 tsp. garlic powder
1 pinch paprika, or as desired

## Directions:

1. Place potatoes into a large pot and cover with salted water; bring to a boil.
2. Reduce heat to medium-low and simmer until tender, 20 to 25 minutes.
3. Drain, cool, and chop potatoes into 1-inch cubes.
4. Combine chopped potatoes and eggs in a large bowl.
5. Mix sour cream, mayonnaise, pimento peppers, green onions, bacon, mustard, sugar, vinegar, salt, black pepper, celery seed, and garlic powder together in a bowl.
6. Pour dressing over potatoes and eggs; toss gently to coat.
7. Sprinkle potato salad with paprika.

# Bacon and Chipotle Potato Salad

## Ingredients:

2 tbsps. chipotle pepper sauce
1 1/2 pounds potatoes, peeled and cut into 1-inch cubes
Salt
3/4 cup sour cream
1/2 cup mayonnaise
1 tbsp. Dijon mustard
1/2 tsp. finely chopped garlic
3 slices bacon, cooked and crumbled
2 hard-cooked eggs, coarsely chopped

## Directions:

1. Place potatoes in a large saucepan and cover with water.
2. Add 2 tsps. salt and bring to a boil.
3. Reduce heat to medium; cover and cook 12 to 15 minutes or until potatoes are tender.
4. Drain and cool.
5. Meanwhile, in a small bowl, combine sour cream, mayonnaise, chipotle sauce, mustard, and garlic; mix well.
6. Place potatoes in a large bowl with bacon and eggs.
7. Add dressing and toss to coat.
8. Season with additional salt, if needed.
9. Cover and refrigerate.

# Bayou Potato Salad

## Ingredients:

2 pounds red potatoes, peeled and quartered
4 hard-cooked eggs
1 cup mayonnaise
1/4 cup Tabasco brand Buffalo Style Hot Sauce
2 tsps. prepared mustard
1 stalk celery, finely chopped
1/3 cup finely chopped green onion

## Directions:

1. Put the potatoes in a large saucepan and cover with water.
2. Bring the potatoes to a boil, reduce heat, and cook until the potatoes are tender, or about 20 minutes.
3. Drain the pot and set the potatoes aside to cool.
4. Cut the eggs in 1/2, place the yolks in a large bowl, and mash the yolks with a fork.
5. Chop the egg whites finely and add to the yolks.
6. Stir in the mayonnaise, Tabasco Buffalo Style Sauce, mustard, celery, and green onion, and mix well.
7. Dice the cooled potatoes and stir into the mayonnaise mixture until well blended.

# Bacon Sriracha Potato Salad

## Ingredients:

3 lbs. red potatoes
3-4 slices of bacon
2 1/2 tbsps. white vinegar
1/4 tsp salt
3/4 cup mayonnaise
1/4 cup sour cream
1.5 tbsp. sriracha chili sauce
1/4 cup chopped green onion
Paprika, to taste

## Directions:

1. Peel potatoes and chop into 3/4-inch cubes.
2. Place potatoes in a large pot and cover with cold water, about 1 inch above the potatoes.
3. Set burner to high and bring water to a boil.
4. Fry bacon until crisp.
5. Once a rolling boil is reached, reduce heat to low and simmer, stirring occasionally, until potatoes are fork tender, about 8 minutes.
6. Drain potatoes and move to a large mixing bowl.
7. Add salt and vinegar and combine gently with a rubber spatula/bowl scraper.
8. Allow to cool slightly, letting the potatoes sit for around 15 minutes.
9. Combine mayonnaise, sour cream, and sriracha chili sauce in a small bowl.
10. Once the potatoes have cooled a bit, fold in the mayonnaise mixture using the rubber spatula.
11. Top with crispy bacon, chopped green onion, and paprika.
12. Serve and enjoy!

# Buffalo Potato Salad

## Ingredients:

2 pounds red potatoes, washed and cut into 1 inch cubes
1/4 cup mayonnaise
1/4 cup Greek yogurt
1/2 cup hot sauce
3 large celery ribs with leafy tops, finely chopped
3 medium carrots, peeled and finely chopped
3 scallions, thinly sliced on a bias
Salt and pepper, to taste

## Directions:

1. Place the potatoes in a large pot.
2. Cover with cold water and bring to a boil over medium-high heat.
3. Cook potatoes 10-12 minutes, until tender.
4. Drain and reserve.
5. In a large mixing bowl, whisk together mayonnaise, yogurt, hot sauce, red onion, celery, carrots, scallions, salt and pepper.
6. Add warm potatoes to the bowl and toss to combine.
7. Cover the bowl with plastic wrap and refrigerate for 2 to 12 hours, stirring occasionally.
8. Serve and enjoy!

# About the Author

Laura Sommers is **The Recipe Lady!**

She lives on a small farm in Baltimore County, Maryland and has a passion for food. She has taken cooking classes in New York City, Memphis, New Orleans and Washington DC. She has been a taste tester for a large spice company in Baltimore and written food reviews for several local papers. She loves writing cookbooks with the most delicious recipes to share her knowledge and love of cooking with the world.

Follow her on Pinterest:

**http://pinterest.com/therecipelady1**

Visit the Recipe Lady's blog for even more great recipes:

**http://the-recipe-lady.blogspot.com/**

Visit her Amazon Author Page to see her latest books:

**amazon.com/author/laurasommers**

Follow the Recipe Lady on Facebook:

**https://www.facebook.com/therecipegirl**

Follow her on Twitter:

**https://twitter.com/TheRecipeLady1**

# Other Books by Laura Sommers

Irish Recipes for St. Patrick's Day

Traditional Vermont Recipes

Traditional Memphis Recipes

Maryland Chesapeake Bay Blue Crab Cookbook

Mussels Cookbook

Maryland Chesapeake Bay Blue Crab Cookbook

Salmon Cookbook

Scallop Recipes

Printed in Poland
by Amazon Fulfillment
Poland Sp. z o.o., Wrocław
11 July 2023

117e6023-cfaf-4acb-be81-2c3885f91e1eR01